Young Heroes

Given Kachepa

Advocate for Human Trafficking Victims

Q.L. Pearce

KIDHAVEN PRESS

An imprint of Thomson Gale, a part of The Thomson Corporation

THOMSON
GALE
™

Detroit • New York • San Francisco • New Haven, Conn. • Waterville, Maine • London

© 2007 Thomson Gale, a part of The Thomson Corporation.

Thomson and Star Logo and KidHaven Press are trademarks and Gale is a registered trademark used herein under license.

For more information, contact:
KidHaven Press
27500 Drake Rd.
Farmington Hills, MI 48331-3535
Or you can visit our Internet site at http://www.gale.com

LIBRARY OF CONGRESS CATALOGING-IN-PUBLICATION DATA

Pearce, Q.L. (Querida Lee)
Given Kachepa / by Q.L. Pearce.
    p. cm.—(Young heroes)
Includes bibliographical references and index.
ISBN: 978-0-7377-3668-7 (hardcover)
1. Kachepa, Given, 1986– 2. Human trafficking victims—Biography—Juvenile literature. 3. Human trafficking—Zambia—Juvenile literature. 4. Human trafficking—United States—Juvenile literature. 5. Children's choirs—Corrupt practices—Juvenile literature. 6. Forced labor—Juvenile literature. I. Title.
HV6250.4.C48P43 2007
362.88—dc22

                                                              2007007779

ISBN-10: 0-7377-3668-2

Printed in the United States of America

Contents

Chapter One

The Land of Promise

Given Kachepa is a long way from his original home in the African nation of Zambia. He came to the United States as a young boy to earn money by singing in a youth choir. Instead he became the victim of modern-day slavery, also known as human trafficking. Nearly half of all human trafficking victims are under the age of eighteen. Given was one of the lucky ones. He was rescued by officers of the U.S. Immigration and Naturalization Service.

On May 2, 2005, Given Kachepa was among ten teens named America's top ten youth volunteers by the Prudential Spirit of Community Awards. He was chosen from a list of more than 20,000 youth volunteers because of his work as an **advocate** for other victims of human trafficking. His goal is to inform and educate the public about this terrible crime and help to bring it to an end.

Life in Africa

Given was born August 20, 1986, in Kalingalinga, a **rural** village near Lusaka, the capital of Zambia. Zambia is one of the poorest nations in the world. Workers in Kalingalinga make about $30 a month. It was hard for Given's parents to feed him and his six brothers and sisters. Their one meal a day usually included whatever could be grown locally, such as corn, beans, pumpkins, or sweet potatoes. A typical meal was *nshima*, which is like mashed potatoes but made from corn and eaten with the bare fingers.

Given went to school without food or lunch money. There was no snack waiting when he returned home from school. There was no running water or electricity in the mud-brick house where his family lived. From

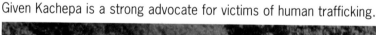

Given Kachepa is a strong advocate for victims of human trafficking.

In Kalingalinga, Zambia, Given's family lived in a mud-brick house.

the time that he was very young, Given knew that he had little chance to get a good education. The best he could expect when he grew up was to find a job that would probably pay no more than a dollar a day.

Poverty was not the only danger that Given and his family faced. Zambia suffers high rates of deadly diseases such as tuberculosis, malaria, and HIV/AIDS. Given's mother died of tuberculosis when he was six years old, and the disease later took his oldest sister, Grace. His father died when Given was nine, leaving the Kachepa children as orphans. "My world fell apart," Given said. "I helped build my father's coffin and remember looking at him thinking he could speak."[1]

Given and his brothers and sisters were able to move in with their Aunt Margret, but she had six children of her own. The two-room house they lived in was made from mud bricks. One room was for his aunt and her husband. The other was for the children. Cousins and brothers and sisters all shared the few blankets. There was no privacy. Every day was a struggle for the large family. At age ten, Given started going straight from school to the bus station to find work. Sometimes he would stand at the bus station for hours hoping to carry a shopper's packages for a few pennies.

"In Kalingalinga you make money however you can,"[2] Given explains. He crushed stones with hammers, burning the top layers of rock with charcoal to soften it. Once he had enough to fill a wheelbarrow, he rolled the heavy load to a place that used the rocks as gravel or to make concrete blocks. The backbreaking work earned him about a dollar a week.

Given found comfort from his difficult life by attending services at the Highland Baptist Church. Christianity is Zambia's official religion.

Given earned money by crushing stones with hammers.

"I used to go to church every Sunday with Bible study and there would be days that I would pray for hours and hours," Given said. "I was excited. I will never forget the day that I [accepted] Jesus Christ [as my savior]. There were things that I did where I could see God working in my life."[3]

The Joy of Song

One of Given's favorite parts of the church service was when the **congregation** would sing hymns. By the time he was ten years old, it was clear that Given had an excellent singing voice. His friends and family encouraged him to join the church choir. After work in the evening, he would go to choir rehearsals before he did his homework. Given loved singing and was happy to have found peace. He said he also believed it was a way to get closer "to God and to my faith."[4]

Not long after he joined the choir, it seemed to Given that his life was about to change for the better. A missionary group called Teaching Teachers to Teach (TTT) came to Zambia to help build schools. The leaders of the group came to Kalingalinga because they had learned of the boys' choir at the church. When Given and the other boys sang, the visitors were impressed. The boys sang a cappella. That means they sang without any musical instruments to accompany them.

Keith Grimes, a member of the missionary organization, was from Sherman, Texas, in the United States. He and his wife spoke excitedly about the many Americans who would love to hear the choir's beautiful songs and would pay to come to concerts. Grimes and his wife explained that they had sponsored choirs before and that the boys and their families would benefit if the youngsters performed in the United States.

The couple claimed that money the choir earned by singing at churches, schools, and malls would be used to build a school in Zambia. Meanwhile the boys would go to school in America and be paid a salary for performing. There would even be enough money to support the families they would leave behind. Given remembers Grimes being very gentle and nicely dressed and seeming trustworthy.

"I could envision nothing bad happening," Given says. "Our parents trusted America as the land of the

Children sing in the African Children's Choir. Given loves to sing and he was initially happy when he was selected to join the choir.

free. If I had stayed, my life would have been a fight. I would have finished [school] through the seventh grade. I would not have a place to stay. I would not know where I would get money for food."[5]

The only thing that stood in the way of Given's trip to America was an audition. The couple planned to take no more than a dozen boys. Given was concerned that he might not be among the lucky few. He had only been singing for two years, and some of the other boys had more experience. There was also a rule that no more than two members of the same family would be chosen. Two of Given's cousins also planned to try out. On the day of the audition, he was very nervous, but he sang his best. He was thrilled when he learned that Grimes made an exception to the rule about family and Given and his cousins, Richard and Mophat, had all been chosen.

"It was like a dream come true," recalled Mophat. "They told us they were going to give us free every-thing—free clothes and money."[6]

Given was eleven years old when he traveled to the United States on May 8, 1998. He was the youngest boy in the choir.

Chapter Two

Living in Fear

In the New Land

Given was thrilled to be making a trip to America. "It was very exciting to be on my first airplane ride. I couldn't sleep the night before we left. I was scared but excited to embark on this new and unfamiliar journey,"[7] Given said. The trip was comfortable, and he thought it was an example of what life was going to be like in America. He knew that there had been other choirs from Zambia that had toured the United States, but he had not been able to speak to any of those boys. He did not learn what had happened to them.

All Given knew was that he would spend at least eighteen months in the land of promise. The boys believed that the United States was a land of wealth and happiness with no crime, poverty, hunger, or loneliness. He would be fed, clothed, educated, and even paid. He would have enough money to send some

Given was the youngest boy in the choir. He is pictured in the top row on the far right.

home to his brothers and sisters. When he returned to Zambia, he would be able to attend the school that he had helped to build.

"To have someone tell you that they could provide what you are missing, you think it is a gift from God,"[8] Given said.

Given's first impression of America was that it was a wonderful country. He was amazed to see many airplanes land at the same time on different runways. The beautiful, well-kept landscape was completely different from what he was used to in Zambia. Given was excited about the future, but his dream soon turned to tragedy.

The promises Grimes had made were lies. Given and the other boys had been tricked. It was true that American audiences were happy to pay to hear the Zambian Boys a Cappella Choir and donate money to build schools, but the funds quickly disappeared into the pockets of their **sponsors**. There were no salaries or checks sent to the families. There was no money for education or schools. The boys had become modern-day slaves, and the nightmare was only beginning.

On the Road

Experts say that a slave is someone who is forced to work without pay and is not free to leave. An estimated 14,500 to 17,500 people are trafficked into the United States every year, and about half are believed to be children. Given soon found himself to be one of these children. He was forced to work eighteen-hour days. He and the other boys spent weeks at a time on tours that took them to as many as 28 states. The twelve choir

For performances, members of the choir had to wear identical African tunics, pants, and shirts. Given often speaks at events wearing a tunic.

members traveled in a fifteen-passenger van, so there was no comfortable way to sleep or rest. The van had air-conditioning and heating, but travel time was unbearable. Sometimes they would drive up to fifteen hours a day, often making several trips per week. If the boys were running late getting to a destination, the driver would not stop for food.

"Sometimes we found ourselves singing one-hour concerts with empty stomachs and little energy,"[9] Given says. Little free time was built into the choir's trips, and recreation was limited to walking around the malls where they performed. Given remembers that while on the road they usually stayed in host homes. "Occasionally we stayed in a motel and that was fun!"[10]

The choir lived in a mobile home similar to this one when they were not on tour.

The choir sang in churches, schools, and malls. The concert schedule was exhausting. Tours lasted from one to six weeks with four to seven concerts a day or as many as twenty concerts a week. If they returned from a perform-ance late at night, they were still expected to get up as early as 4:30 A.M. to travel to the next performance site. Given says, "Sometimes, I just slept in my clothes because I was too tired and knew I had to be ready to go so early in the morning. I was still expected to smile and be friendly when I arrived to set up to sing at each performance."[11]

While on tour each boy was responsible for keeping his own clothes washed and pressed. The choir wore identical African tunics, shirts, and pants that the TTT Ministry had brought from Africa. The outfit was **mandatory** on stage or when visiting with host families. The boys also had to set up the microphones and speak-ers, test the equipment, and then take it down for each concert. They sang songs in English as well as Nyanja, Bemba, Tonga, and other Zambian languages. "Soon and Very Soon" and "Mupati Mupati" (He's Great, He's Great) were two of the songs they often sang.

Conditions at Home

When the choir was not on tour, they lived in Whites-boro, Texas, in a mobile home. They slept in a single room in bunk beds. They washed and ironed their own clothes, cooked their own food, and cleaned. A typical meal was *nshima* served with some kind of vegetable, meat, or soup. There was little time to relax. Sometimes they entertained themselves with soccer and basketball.

After weeks of this routine, Given felt that nothing was fun anymore. Even his precious music did not bring joy, because he had to sing so much.

Then the ministry decided it would be nice for the choir to have a swimming pool. The boys were very excited, until they learned they had to dig the hole for the pool themselves. Even in the sweltering July heat, the digging was mandatory. Mornings began with a run, then they would dig until breakfast. Because of their travel schedule, the pool was never finished. Given later learned that the hole was eventually used as a dump for gifts from host families such as shoes, clothes, CDs, cassettes, pictures, books, letters, and Bibles that the ministry had taken away from the choir members.

False Promises

In spite of the hardships, Given and his friends continued to sing, hoping the money they were earning was helping their families out of poverty. "After about three months we began to ask questions about what we had been told in Zambia," Given said. "When we demanded for answers about the money and school, Mr. Grimes became very angry."[12]

Grimes was familiar with Zambian customs. He knew that the boys had been taught to obey and respect their elders. He denied that he had promised to send Given and his friends to school. Grimes claimed the education he had promised was the experience of traveling, meeting new people, and seeing new places. It became clear that he did not intend to supply books or

Given stares out of the TTT offices.

pay the choir a salary. The promises that had been made in Zambia were broken.

Since the first choir group had visited the United States in 1993, TTT had sold tapes and **solicited** donations, telling audiences that they were building a school in Zambia for the returning singers. The producer of the audiotapes for the first choir claimed that they had earned $250,000 in only three months. The money, however, was not used as promised.

Given could see the donation baskets filled with cash, but when the boys asked about money, Grimes would question how Christian boys could do that. He said that if they were Christians, they would not be thinking about money. The ministry officials regularly read the boys scripture about rebellion, being obedient, discipline, fear, the love of money, and being a servant.

Fear and Silence

Given remembers that Keith Grimes and his son-in-law, Gary Martens, were both short-tempered. He said:

> When they yelled at me or spoke to me in a voice that was mad, I felt scared and humiliated. I personally experienced Keith Grimes's hot temper during a very long performance day. We had already sung about eight performances and still had more to go. I was very, very tired and sat down to rest. Mr. Grimes came over to me and told me to stand and get ready to sing. I told him I was very tired. He grabbed me by the shirt, stood me up and said loudly in my face, "I said get up and sing, boy. Unless you want to go home, you will sing."[13]

The boys were often threatened with **deportation**, which was viewed as a sign that a choir member had been disrespectful to his American elders. In Zambia, being deported meant disgrace to a boy's family and his community. The choir member who was deported would become an outcast and might even lose his place in his own family's home.

The fear of deportation made Given and his fellow choir members keep quiet about their plight when they stayed with host families on the road. They were not allowed to ask questions, use the phone, or accept any gifts. If a friend tucked a gift into a choir member's luggage, ministry officials, who routinely searched travel bags, would take it. Like all of the singers, Given was trained about what to say in case a host family became suspicious and called investigators. Several of the boys became seriously ill when the youngsters were even denied medical care, but still they were afraid to complain.

"The problem is the traffickers are very good at controlling their victims," says Wade Horn, assistant secretary for children and families with the Department of Health and Human Services. "Getting the message [that help is available] directly to the victims is difficult."[14] The ministry told the boys that no one would be willing to help them in the United States. "Human trafficking is so hidden you don't know who you're fighting—the victims are so scared, they're not going to tell you what's happening to them,"[15] said Given. He explains that they were not fenced in or chained, but they

The choir members were often threatened with deportation.

were miles from a big city. The boys believed that running away was useless because the neighbors would not help them. The ministry held their passports and listened to their phone calls. Whenever Given received a letter, it was always opened by the ministry office. He knew that pictures, money, and phone cards had been taken. Given learned not to trust anyone.

"I lost hope while I was held captive," he says. "My traffickers used tactics that made me feel like I was a worthless individual and told me no one would have any interest in helping me. I felt hopelessness and blamed myself for everything. . . . I felt like a puppet on a string being moved around."[16] Given wondered if he would ever be rescued.

Chapter Three

Rescue

Discovery

Things began to change after a performance in Missouri. Given felt too sick to sing, and he was sent home under the threat of deportation. Later the choir decided that if he was deported, they would all go. They felt they needed to stand together for what was right. To punish them, Gary Martens disconnected the gas cooking stove in their living quarters so they could not cook that day. The message was "no singing, no food."

Some of the boys began to rebel. They refused to sing without food. They secretly taped conversations, saved contact information from host homes, and became more open about their mistreatment. In spite of the threats, they were no longer willing to accept their terrible situation.

In 1999, Keith Grimes died of a brain tumor. His daughter, Barbara Grimes Martens, took control of the choir and continued to run

The INS helped remove Given and the rest of the choir from the ministry.

it as her father had. She decided to deport some boys to set an example for the rest. She called the police to take two boys, Samson and Boston, away. After talking to the two choir members, the police reported the case to the Immigration and Naturalization Service (INS) and the U.S. Department of Labor.

Agent Salvador Orrantia arrived at the ministry. A soft-spoken man, he put Samson and Boston into the INS car and drove away. The rest of the boys huddled in their beds, some crying. Now twelve years old, Given was frightened and confused.

"This terrified me," he admitted. "I thought the same thing was going to happen to me."[17] The next morning, Orrantia showed up again and took two more boys, Given's cousin Mophat and a boy named Martin. For Given, it was one of the worst things he had ever experienced. "That felt like someone had just stabbed a knife inside me saying, 'I own you and I can do whatever I want with you.'"[18]

He had no way of knowing that the four boys taken by the INS were not being returned to Zambia. The INS had placed them in temporary homes while the case was investigated. Several host families were interviewed as a part of the inquiry, and former attorney general Janet Reno had been sent letters about the **allegations.**

Through another Zambian boy, Given learned that Mophat was not only still in the United States, but he was in a host home and enrolled in a real school. The Zambian boy had seen Mophat and Martin at a store in town. They had given the boy their phone numbers.

The choir was soon on tour again, but because of the investigation, things were different. The INS and the Department of Labor instructed the ministry to pay the choir for singing. The ministry obeyed, but then began charging the boys for their food, clothing, and rent.

Once he returned to Whitesboro, Given called Mophat and asked what had happened to him. Given was amazed to learn from his cousin that there was a chance of rescue. He shared the news with the other boys, and the choir decided to quit singing. They were able to reach the INS and asked to be removed from the ministry. Orrantia returned and picked up every remaining choir member. On a brisk day in January 2000, the long ordeal appeared to be coming to an end.

A Helping Hand

Sandy Shepherd was a member of the First Baptist Church of Colleyville in Texas. She had never seen Given's choir perform, but she was familiar with the TTT Ministry. Shepherd had been a volunteer when her church had hosted an earlier choir Keith Grimes had brought from Zambia. Even then, she had sensed that something was wrong. She had called the Federal Bureau of Investigation to complain that the boys were being **exploited**, unaware that they were actually the victims of human trafficking.

She was happy to help when Orrantia called the church and asked if they could find temporary homes for the boys in the choir. He had no place to put them, and he knew that taking them to a holding cell would only worry them. Shepherd remembers arriving at the church to find seven frightened boys standing in a circle with two INS officers. She soon found homes for all of them, and Given left to stay with a family in western Texas.

"It was extremely difficult to trust anyone at the time," he said. "Unfortunately, I was trafficked during the years when most kids are learning to trust and figuring out themselves."[19]

A New Home

When Given's new foster mom was unable to continue to care for him because of her poor health, Sandy Shepherd

Given sits with Sandy and Deetz Shepherd. Sandy stepped in to help and found homes for the boys in the choir.

and her husband, Deetz, stepped in again. Their children were going to college and there was plenty of room, so Given moved into the Shepherd home and started school.

Given worked and studied hard in the eighth grade. He had already missed two years of school, and the language barrier was a challenge. Getting back in the routine of homework was difficult, but he had help from his new family. His love of music returned and he soon joined the school choir.

Given found a new home with the Shepherd family.

By the time he entered Grapevine High School, Given felt more at home. He became active in the theater program and in sports. "I played soccer for three years and ran cross country for two years. . . . I have fun memories of high school and would not exchange that experience for anything in the world,"[20] Given said.

The most important change was that Given realized he was where he belonged. "They [the Shepherds] love me and care a lot about me. I am very blessed and honored to be living with them."[21]

In the spring of 2002, the Shepherds went to court and became Given's legal guardians. At nineteen, Given was granted a **visa** and certified human trafficking victims status.

Taking another critical step in the healing process, Given says: "I learned how to forgive. My faith in God is my guiding rod. . . . Because I have forgiven my traffickers, the burden of my past has been lifted. . . . I have moved past the time in my life when I was a victim, and now I am a survivor of human trafficking."[22]

Given feels that he did not actively decide to stay in the United States. He says:

It was for God who worked through people like mom Sandy Shepherd and Sal Orrantia of the INS that I was able to stay. These people put so much effort and energy into us and made sure that we were well taken care of. God provided all this because he wanted me to accomplish my goal of helping my family and finishing my education. I am glad God chose that path for me, I am living my dream.[23]

Given graduated from Grapevine High School. He had missed two years of school when he was with the ministry, so he had to study hard to catch up.

All but four of the choir members remained in the United States. Given remains in touch with most of them, particularly his cousins Richard and Mophat. He is also in close touch with his family in Zambia. He calls them regularly and hopes that someday he can return to visit.

A Closing Chapter

The ministry that had brought the boys to America was dissolved in January of 2000 when the INS removed the choir from TTT custody. Although the federal government knew that Keith Grimes's ministry was involved in human trafficking, they could not have brought

Given speaks out about human trafficking to increase awareness.

charges because the federal anti–human trafficking law was not yet in effect. Still, almost $1 million in penalties was levied against TTT.

Barbara Grimes Martens eventually moved from Texas. She continues to claim that all of the allegations are false.

Chapter Four

An Advocate for Victims

Given is happy in his new home. His mom explains that although he has experienced many terrible things that children should not have to endure, he has become a polite, respectful, and caring young man.

"He is a delight to have around the house. He sings a lot of the time," she says. "Given is caught between two continents with loyalty and love for a family. It is a hard place to be at times. As he became a survivor in his mind, his attitude about life changed and he realized that he could help others understand the **atrocity** of human trafficking."[24]

Given is described by friends and family as humble, kind, honest, and hardworking. He regularly sends money home to his brothers and sisters in Zambia for food, medicine, clothes, and school. He believes that it is not what you look like, but who you are as a person that matters.

Given stands in his bedroom in his new home.

Given attends college in Texas. He is studying biology. He does extremely well in his work and earns excellent grades. He attends church regularly and goes to a weekly Bible study session on campus. Given feels that life in college is challenging but fun. He enjoys learning and making new friends and finding out more about his own weaknesses and strengths.

"I would like to become a dentist," he says. "But this is a process. If this is what God has planned for me then it will happen, if not then He will choose another path for me."[25]

Speaking Out

When not in school, Given travels around the nation making audiences aware of human trafficking. He has spoken at dozens of schools, churches, and business organizations.

"From the moment I met him, Given impressed me with his quiet confidence and humbled me with his resolve to end slavery around the world and especially in his native Zambia,"[26] says Kevin Bales of Free the Slaves.

Since his rescue, Given's story has been told in newspapers and magazines and on television, radio, and the

Given is shown here in his dorm room. He attends college in Texas.

Internet. He has even testified at hearings to help pass antitrafficking laws that help victims and punish traffickers.

For his hard work and dedication, Given has received several high honors, including the Hitachi Foundation Yoshiyama Award for community service, the Ronald McDonald Future Achievers for Black Students, and the Field Scovell Scholarship. Given was recently recognized in the April issue of *Teen People* as one of "20 Teens Who Will Change the World." Congressman Kenny Marchant says of Given, "He is an in-

Given speaks about human trafficking at schools around the country.

spiring example of a young person who has made a major difference in the life of others."[27]

Given is still a little bewildered by all of the attention he has received since his rescue. He hopes to use it to make people aware of the horrors of trafficking. "In my heart, I resolved to help rid the world of the human trafficking," Given explains. "I do not want anyone else to suffer the mental **brutality** and psychological **trauma** victims endure. I feel traffickers should receive punishment for abusing lives of other people for their own benefit."[28]

Given has found in his travels that most people do not know a single thing about human trafficking. When he talks about trafficking, most audiences cannot believe that it can happen in America. They believe slavery was eliminated long ago, and they are shocked to learn that more slaves exist today that at any other time in human history.

Slavery Affects Us All

Given believes that society should educate children as well as adults about human trafficking. "It's important that we all respect and value one another. If we do just that then we will be fine. Human beings are not disposable."[29]

Young people may feel that slavery is too serious a problem for them to solve. Still, there are things that youngsters can do. For example, choosing wisely at the supermarket can make a difference. Certain products sold in stores may be made or harvested by slave labor. When products such as coffee, tea, sugar, and chocolate are labeled "Fair Trade Certified," they are guaranteed to be from workers who received fair wages. Nonfood products that may be produced by slave labor include cotton, steel, oriental rugs, diamonds, and silk.

A Special Day

Free the Slaves.org has established February 27 as Anti-Slavery Day. It is a time to focus attention on the 27 million slaves around the world. Encourage friends and family to recognize the day and what it stands for.

One way to draw attention to the plight of the world's slaves is to write a letter of protest about trafficking to a government representative, or to the school or local newspaper. An excellent activity for a group is to create and pass out fact sheets about human traffick-

Given has received several high honors, including the Field Scovell Scholarship.

A package of coffee beans displays a "Fair Trade Certified" label.

ing to friends and family members. Young people could also organize a **vigil** to show support or to remember those affected by slavery. Invite friends and family to gather and light a candle for the world's slaves.

The most important thing that young people can do is to add their unique voice to the chorus of people who refuse to allow human trafficking to continue. Kevin Bales of Free the Slaves stated: "Criminals are clever, and most citizens can't see slavery even when it is in front of them. We desperately need voices like Given's to help America see the slavery that is hidden in plain sight."[30]

Notes

Chapter One: The Land of Promise

1. Given Kachepa, interview with the author, January 5, 2007.
2. Kachepa interview.
3. Quoted in John Celock, "Surreal Slave Song," BustedHalo.com. www.busted halo. com/features/HumanTrafficking part2.htm.
4. Quoted in Celock, "Surreal Slave Song."
5. Quoted in John Celock, "Slavery Under- cover," Children's Voice.com, July/August 2006. www.cwla.org/voice/0607slavery.htm.
6. Quoted in A Capella News, January 9, 2004. www.acappellanews.com/archive/000221.html.

Chapter Two: Living in Fear

7. Kachepa interview.
8. Quoted in Celock, "Surreal Slave Song."
9. Kachepa interview.
10. Kachepa interview.
11. Kachepa interview.
12. Kachepa interview.
13. Kachepa interview.
14. Quoted in Associated Press, "Human Traf- ficking Becomes an Elusive Target in the U.S.," *USA Today*, October 29, 2005. www. usatoday.com/news/nation/2005-10-29- ushumantrafficking_x.htm.

15. Quoted in Associated Press, "Human Trafficking Becomes an Elusive Target in the U.S."
16. Quoted in Barbara Kralis, "Trafficking in Your Own Backyard," RenewAmerica. www.renewamerica.us/columns/kralis/060801.

Chapter Three: Rescue

17. Kachepa interview.
18. Given Kachepa, Application for T Nonimmigrant (T-1) Status, granted August 2003.
19. Kachepa interview.
20. Kachepa interview.
21. Given Kachepa, Application for T Nonimmigrant (T-1) Status, granted August 2003.
22. Quoted in Kralis, "Trafficking in Your Own Backyard."
23. Kachepa interview.

Chapter Four: An Advocate for Victims

24. Sandy Shepherd, interview with the author, January 12, 2007.
25. Kachepa interview.
26. Quoted in Free the Slaves, "20 Teens Who Will Change the World," January 23, 2006. http://freetheslaves.net/slavery/.
27. Quoted in United States House of Representatives, "Marchant Announces Award for Grapevine High School Student," May 17, 2005. www.house.gov/list/press/tx24_marchant/studentvolunteer.html.
28. Quoted in BlackNews.com, "*Teen People* Celebrates the 8th Annual '20 Teens Who Will Change

the World.'" www.blacknews.com/pr/teenpeople
101.html.

29. Kachepa interview.

30. Quoted in BlackNews.com, *Teen People* Celebrates the 8th Annual '20 Teens Who Will Change
the World.'"

Glossary

advocate: Somebody who speaks in support of something.

allegations: An accusation of wrongdoing yet to be proven.

atrocity: A cruel act of violence against another.

brutality: Cruel, harsh behavior.

congregation: A group of people gathered for a religious service.

deportation: The forced removal of a foreign person from a country.

exploited: To be treated unfairly for someone else's personal gain.

mandatory: Required, must be done.

rural: In or around the country.

solicited: Requested or pleaded for something.

sponsors: People who take responsibility for someone else.

trauma: Severe shock caused by a terrible experience.

vigil: A period of waiting, watching, or guarding.

visa: An official document to enter or leave a country.

For Further Exploration

Book

Shirlee Newman, *Child Slavery in Modern Times*. Danbury, CT: Franklin Watts, 2000. This book gives an overview of the plight of present-day child slaves in homes, fields, and factory sweatshops of the United States. It includes photographs and personal narratives of many young victims of human trafficking.

Web Sites

The American Anti-Slavery Group (www.antislavery. org/). A U.S.-based nonprofit group dedicated to the abolition of modern-day slavery. The site includes essays and current news about slavery, as well as information on how to take action for change.

Fair Trade Products (www.transfairusa.org/). Information about Fair Trade Certified products with producer profiles and links to locations that carry the products. Other resources include fast facts, press releases, and media highlights.

Free the Children (www.freethechildren.com/index. php). Free the Children is a network of children helping children. Information includes how to start a youth action group, adopt a village, or build a school. Educational materials include short videos and "Ask the Professor," a place where children can get answers to their questions about poverty, inequality, globalization, and human rights.

Free the Slaves (http://freetheslaves.net/resources/k12/). Activities and worksheets for upper elementary and middle grade students. The site includes many photos, research documents, victims' stories, suggestions for taking action, and a store that offers books and videos.

Rugmark.org (www.rugmark.org/home.php). A site dedicated to ending child labor in the rug and carpet industry. It includes children's profiles, a slide show, information on opportunities for rescued children, news and events, and sources for handwoven rugs that are certified Child-Labor-Free.

If you observe a situation that looks like it could involve human trafficking, call the national trafficking hotline at 1-888-373-7888. To learn more about modern slavery, visit www.freetheslaves.net.

Index

Picture Credits

About the Author

Q.L. Pearce has written more than 100 trade books for children and more than 30 classroom workbooks and teacher manuals on the topics of reading, science, math, and values. Pearce has written science-related articles for magazines; regularly gives presentations at schools, bookstores, and libraries; and is a frequent contributor to the educational program of the Los Angeles County Fair. She is the assistant regional advisor for the Society of Children's Book Writers and Illustrators in Orange, San Bernardino, and Riverside counties and is a member of the advisory board for Cal State Fullerton's Writing for Children program.